Church Folks vs. Christians
Do You See the Difference?

Michelle Coleman Anderson

Copyright © 2025 Michelle Coleman Anderson

All rights reserved.

Scripture quotations marked KJV are taken from *The Holy Bible*, King James Version; those marked NKJV are taken from *The Holy Bible*, New King James Version. Copyright © 2019, 2021 by Thomas Nelson, Inc. Used by permission. All rights reserved.

Scripture quotations marked NIV are taken from *The Holy Bible*, New International Version. Copyright © 2018 by Zondervan Corporation. Used by permission. All rights reserved.

ISBN-13: 979-8-218-84325-0

DEDICATIONS

This book is dedicated to my loving, supportive family and the special memories of my grandmothers, Homer Lee Foster and Daisy Gilkey, and my cousin, Carol "Jackie" Smith.

CONTENTS

	Acknowledgments	i
	Foreword	ii
Chapter 1	Introducing the Problem	1
Chapter 2	Typical "Church Folks"	6
Chapter 3	There is a Difference	17
Chapter 4	That Little Tongue	26
Chapter 5	So Busy	43
Chapter 6	The "I" in "Church"	56
Chapter 7	Synthetic Saint	65
Chapter 8	One-Night Stand	77
Chapter 9	What's In You?	88
Chapter 10	The Winning Side	98

ACKNOWLEDGMENTS

All praise goes to God first! Additionally, I would like to express heartfelt gratitude to the following people:

- My husband, Gussie Anderson, and our four kiddos (aka "The Clan") for keeping me calm, laughing, uplifted, grounded, and motivated (to say the least)
- My parents, Willie and Lillie Coleman for being exemplary role models; my siblings Terry and Janelle plus my aunts and cousins for being loving and supportive
- My late pastor, the one and only "Son of Thunder" Rev. Dr. Charles Polk, Sr., and my very special St. Luther Church family for their spiritual nurturing
- The incomparable late Pastor Thomas Bernard, for his rich insight over the years and contribution
- My cousin, Germaine, for his kind investment in this work
- Kendra King, for her awesome book cover design
- Professors Preselfannie McDaniels and C. Liegh McInnis for their feedback and guidance

FOREWORD

For several years now, I have watched Michelle as she showed great care and frustration concerning the church and people who bear the name Christian. Being my daughter-in-law, a believer, and a musician like myself, I understand that she has faced some challenges while dealing with, teaching, and inspiring choir members and others affiliated with the church.

While it is lamentable, it should not be surprising that everybody in the church is not for the church. A cross around our necks and a bible under our arms does not mean that we are on our way to heaven. If we go to heaven we will not get there ANYHOW. Matthew 5:8 announces "Blessed are the pure in heart: for they shall see God" (NIV).

Statistics dictate that the average church consists of more sinners than saints, more fakers than faithful, more liars than true believers, more devilish deceivers than determined disciples, and more people on their way to hell than on the narrow road to heaven. It is estimated that about 25% of church members are saved, 65% are lost and 10% don't know who they are.

What is the difference between a church member and a Christian? There is a vast difference between churchanity and Christianity. The reason why a large percentage of church goers are all churched out is because churchanity was never designed to keep you satisfied, but searching (church to church, city to city, denomination to denomination) and looking for a spiritual fix instead of a spiritual experience with the Savior. Churchanity is fashioned after the traditions of men while Christianity is birthed from the will of GOD.

Church Folks vs. Christians makes one think about this problem and carefully consider a solution. The fact is that Michelle's discovery about the church's state of being is more of a revelation than a fickle fact. While religion has always operated separately from Christianity, church members have tended to put more emphasis on and design "churching" around their methods rather than the message and mission of Jesus Christ. From flushing out church folk in chapter 2 of this book to measuring up the bona fide Christian in chapter 10, Michelle makes it certainly clear that the real destiny of every believer should be pleasing God by striving to live a holy life.

The book reminds me of a sermon I once preached

entitled, "The Danger of Churchanity." The point of the message was that a church goer could go to church every Sunday, teach Sunday school, sing in the choir, wear a deacon's badge, or grace the pulpit, decked out in holistic attire, and still not be a bona fide Christian. I was both inspired and convicted as I slowly turned the pages of this book knowing that we all must one day stand before the righteous judge and give an account of our stewardship, whether it is good or bad. I recommend this book to you and encourage you to read it with sincerity of heart and hope that it will bless you and deepen your spiritual walk with God.

Thomas E. Bernard, Pastor

Travelers Rest Baptist Church

Vicksburg, Mississippi

1 INTRODUCING THE PROBLEM

Picture this: one evening, while driving in unfamiliar territory, you get lost and decide to stop somewhere nearby for directions. You pull up in front of a building and hurriedly walk inside without glancing around to see what type of building it is. Apparently, a meeting is taking place and you have just walked into the midst of a very heated discussion. You see that there is a significant number of people attending the meeting. Everyone, except the three people standing in front of the crowd having a yelling match, turns to look at you when you walk in. Yet, only two or three individuals greet you kindly with a nod of the head or a slight smile. Immediately, all of the attention turns back to the individuals who are up talking.

Not wanting to disturb the meeting, you decide to leave and try to get directions somewhere else. Before turning around to walk back out, you notice that some attendees have scowls on their faces and are rolling their eyes at the people up front. Some people, looking dismayed, are simply staring down at the floor. Others sit with smirks on their faces, looking around the room at everyone else. Still, others are sitting nonchalantly, with blank expressions and folded arms. All of a sudden, to your surprise, a couple of individuals get up and stomp out. You quickly turn on your heels and walk out, feeling a bit disturbed and still lacking the directions you need. Basically, you end up leaving that building in the same state you originally entered in. As you begin driving off, you notice a weak light on the side of the building, flickering as if it could go out at any time. To your horror, this pathetic source of light reveals a small sign with a cross on it, indicating that this building is a church. What a shock and definitely a shame!

If one ever travels to or through Mississippi, he or she would not be able to deny the fact that there is a church on almost every street. In some instances, there are more than three churches within a mile of each other; there is one particular street in Jackson where three churches sit in a row, with another church sitting across the street. The United States Census Bureau revealed that there are close to three million people residing in Mississippi and over one million of these individuals make up the Baptist, United Methodist, and Roman Catholic denominations, which are primary religions in Mississippi. It seems like a great number of Mississippians know God, right?

Despite the overwhelming number of Mississippi residents who comprise the various religious denominations, there is a great decline, statewide and nationwide, in the amount of people who are affiliated with a church. According to a very informative article that can be found at www.intothyword.org, The Francis A. Schaeffer Institute of Church Leadership and Development and Dr. Richard J. Krejcir present the statistics and reasons for church decline in the United States. Extensive research on this topic began around 1992, with The Schaeffer Institute picking this project up around 1998. Researchers basically affirmed that "God's marvelous church has become culturally irrelevant and even distant from its prime purpose of knowing him, growing in Him, and worshipping Him by making disciples" (2007).

The statistics and points brought out in this article are both astounding and alarming to me. I am disquieted by the various reasons people are straying away from the church. There are numerous reasons why some people choose to stop going to church, but Dr. Krejcir mentions certain ones. One reason ascribed to the decline in church attendance is pain; this pain can stem from betrayal, disrespect, a misuse of power, and so on. At any rate, hurt people are leaving the church. Now, from what I grew up hearing, the church is supposed to be the hospital for the hurt and sick. Why then are injured people leaving the hospital that was established to nurse their wounds? Aside from hurt, sometimes there is resentment; this bitterness usually builds up over time. With resentment comes disrespect, anger, and, in extreme cases, violence. It really does not matter if the cause of the pain and resentment is a one-time offense, or a string of offenses, alienation is many times the end result. This is definitely a reason as to why large numbers of church parking lots are looking skimpier and skimpier each week.

According to the Pew Forum, there are over two billion Christians on the planet; this accounts for about a third of the total population of Earth. This is an enormous number; however, there is no guarantee that every one of these individuals understands the accountability and urgency that surrounds living a Christian lifestyle. This manuscript is intended to communicate this urgency and bring to light the real accountability Christians have.

My intended audience is primarily every individual who considers him or herself to be a Christian. Christians have a huge responsibility to the world and, more importantly, to God. Additionally, it is my hope that unbelievers will also inspect the words of this text. I will make several arguments about the differences between bona fide Christians and the counterfeit Christians that populate many of our church buildings today. There are recognizable differences in mannerisms, speech, and mindsets, among other things. Knowledge about these differences, along with a fresh determination to work harder at pleasing God, is what I hope readers will take away with them. As a result, maybe church folks will become less successful at running people away from the church and more successful at bringing the unsaved into the fold.

2 TYPICAL "CHURCH FOLKS"

Over the years, many times, I have either heard or said myself that "Church is not funny, but some of the people in the church are!" This statement usually comes to mind when there is a discussion about all of the drama that sometimes goes on in the church; unfortunately, the drama is increasing. Let us take the opening situation, for example. You walk right into the middle of an argument taking place in the church. You enter the building, barely greeted in any type of loving manner. You observe negative behavior and you witness a lack of respect for God's house and the authority figure conducting the meeting. Most importantly, you leave the building feeling bad and in the exact same lost, confused state you entered in. To top it off, the light that is supposed to illuminate from the church is almost completely gone out. Does this draw a picture of our churches today?

Many times, in various conversations, comments are made about how sad it is that we "saved folks" cannot get along. You have heard the stories about the different issues that go on in some of our churches today; these issues are pointless, which is what makes church folks seem so "funny." Let us start with the music ministry; I know this area all too well, and it can be full of drama! Besides, it is a well-known fact that the devil was a part of this ministry, so it is no surprise that, even today, there are still problems in this area. In Music Department A, the organist and the pianist are squabbling over who should have the title of Minister of Music. In Music Department B, Ms. Lady is furious with Mr. Man because he leads more songs than she does. In Music Department C, the choir members live any kind of way throughout the week, but have attitudes because the members of the congregation don't shout all over the church when they sing on Sunday morning.

Of course, the music department is not the only place where drama lurks; it flows throughout all of the departments in the church and even crawls into the pulpit at times. At Church A, the former usher board president is making waves because the current president does not run the department the exact same way she did. In Church B, the First Lady is deterring people from coming to church with her bossiness and nosiness. Some of the female members of Church C are jealous of the attention that the pastor's wife receives. In one congregation, the deacons are frustrating the pastor with their beliefs that they run the church. In another congregation, the pastor is irritating some of the members because he repeatedly shows favoritism to a select group. Still, in another congregation, some of the older members are annoyed because the newly elected pastor has made some changes that interrupt their "traditional" ways of doing things. I could go on and on with different scenarios and situations, but you get the point. Even though these are simply examples, rest assured, where there are church folks, there is some form of mess.

Regardless of what type of "church drama" is being discussed on the radio, beauty shop, or inside the church, the opening statement comes to mind. One day, though, instead of laughing at church folks and their silliness, I really thought about the implications for a minute. This time, the statement actually bothered me because, in my mind, people who are members of God's church should get along. There should not be any mess in the church; of course, the reality is that many churches are full of it! The bigger reality is that we, the so-called Christians, bring the mess into the church…how else does it get there? Well, once I really thought this through, something dawned on me- yes, church folks are sometimes messy, but real Christians are not; there is a big difference between the two. Things started making sense to me; when we are bickering over little stuff and disturbing the church, we are not behaving as Christians, but merely as church folks. Once this concept hit me, I began to ask myself: do I normally behave like one of those church folks? What about you?

I will be the first to truthfully admit to you that I am not perfect and will never be; neither will you. In fact, we are not even good! Mark 10:18 tells us that Jesus said, "There is none good but one; that is God" (NIV). However, I just do not believe Jesus intended for us to use this statement as an excuse; I am sorry that we cannot sit on this scripture as a comfortable cushion. We are to still strive for perfection on a daily basis. According to Matthew 5:48, Jesus continues "Be ye therefore perfect, even as your Father which is in heaven is perfect" (KJV). I know some people may say this is contradictory, but it is not. God knows that we are not perfect nor are we even good; therefore, we cannot reach perfection and God does not expect us to. Reaching perfection is not humanly possible, yet, every day, we are to strive to be as perfect, pure, and holy as humanly possible. 2 Timothy 3:17 states, "That the man of God may be perfect, thoroughly furnished unto all good works" (KJV). What I get from this verse is that Christians, the men and women of God, can be ideal examples for the world to follow because God fully equips us to do good works and be good models. Furthermore, although we are not good, we are instructed to attempt to do good and model good behavior. This is pleasing to God and should be a true Christian's sole focus.

Speaking of the Christian's sole focus, do you really know what a Christian is? I am sure you are probably thinking, "Is she kidding; who does not know what a Christian is?" Yes, you have heard this term thrown about here and there, probably for many years now, but I am not so sure everyone really knows how much accountability and responsibility is entangled in this word. Over the years, I have found that we use this expression very loosely; we use it too loosely to be honest. People tend to use the terms "church folk" and "Christians" interchangeably; I have remembered times when I have done so. This is a mistake! Yes, contrary to what you may think or believe, church folks and Christians are not the same. By the close of the final chapter, I hope to have made the differences between these two groups clear.

Well, if true Christians solely focus on pleasing God as well as living as Jesus did, what do church folks focus on? It seems like the typical church folks I have encountered focus on everything else! Why do I say this? It appears to me that church folks do not fully comprehend the duties and expectations of the church. The church has more to do than have programs and raise money; we have a bigger calling on our lives than simply wearing titles and holding positions. There is a call to the church to serve others, lead sinners to Christ, and be loving and sincere in doing so.

A major problem with church folks' focus is that it is not in the right place. It should be on important, sensible things, but, oddly, it is on the unimportant things that really serve no purpose. Nowadays, it seems that what is at the forefront of most church folks' minds is concern about recognition, reputation, programs, and size, to name a few things. Most of the time, within the church realm, all you hear about is who dresses the sharpest, whose name gets called the most, whose ministry is the best, which congregation is the largest, which church has the biggest edifice, and so on. These concepts are not completely irrelevant, but certainly should not be main concerns among church people. There are too many real issues that need to be addressed and souls that need to be saved. The present state of the world is chaotic and the church should be engaged in fighting real wars such as teen pregnancy, violence, homosexuality, and suicide, to name a few issues. It is up to the church to fight a victorious spiritual war; however, this cannot be done with the wrong mindset and erroneous focus.

Now, based on what has been covered so far, there may be an unclear perception of what I mean when I discuss typical church folks; let us pause for a minute so that I can clarify. Am I saying that every person who attends church and is concerned with programs or holding a position is not a Christian? Am I saying that every person who gets involved in an altercation is definitely not saved? No, this is not what I mean at all. The church folks I am referring to in this text are those who routinely attend church, stir up trouble while there, blab on and on about nothing, focus their attention on vain matters, and knowingly contribute zilch to the building up of God's kingdom.

This brings about another question you may want

to ask: am I saying that a true Christian never causes problems and always contributes to kingdom building? No; based on my understanding of Christianity, I am saying that a true Christian does not purposely cause problems in the church and tries to always contribute, one way or another, to the building up of the kingdom. Because we are not Jesus, we will not go through life mistake-free and faultless, but, because we are to be *like* Jesus, we are to try hard to come as close to flawless as possible. We are to ensure that our hearts are compassionate, our motives are pure, and our minds are fixated on righteousness. Ah hah…Now you are starting to get it, right?

As I began really exploring the dissimilarities between church folks and Christians, I became more and more amazed at how much I was missing the mark at actually living up to the prestigious title I had been claiming for so many years. I then began to wonder just how many other people had never thought about this concept. How many more people were just claiming Christianity without fulfilling the terms of the title? What I mean is we do not always see ourselves the way we really are; therefore, we are not aware of every gesture and facial expression we make or every word and phrase we say. Think about this:

whether you love taking pictures or not, there are just some photos of you that do not do you justice. The reasons vary: you may look too dark, you may look too big, you may have been distracted by someone or something else, or maybe you were just not ready when the camera flashed. No matter what the case, some pictures just do not come out right.

Think of this book as a collection of photographs capturing how you look, sound, think, and act. You may see dark pictures of yourself-these are the times when you act ugly, say mean things, or display jealousy, bitterness, or hatred. You may see pictures of yourself looking large-these are the times when you are puffed up in pride or think more highly of yourself than you ought to. You may see portraits of yourself looking distracted-these are the times when you are slack on reading and meditating on God's word; during these times you allow the devil to distract you and take your focus off of God. Regardless of how you see yourself, I just want you to get a glimpse of how you behave and speak most of the time. I am confident that you will be amazed at what you observe about yourself. I most definitely was, and, as I stated earlier, am still amazed at how often I resemble one of those church folks discussed in this work.

Just to be clear though, this book is not written as an attempt to bash other people, pass judgment, or criticize anyone; it is not my goal to point my finger at another person or act like I am holier than thou, because, I cannot. The word is clear when it says, in Romans 3:23, "For all have sinned and come short of the glory of God" (KJV). Since I fall into the category of "all," I know I am not excluded. Well, then what is my motive for writing this? It is to simply shed light on how we sometimes come across to others, specifically those outside of the body of Christ. We don't always "represent" God right. This can and should be corrected; it is my sincere hope that this manuscript will help all of us who profess to be Christians actually realize the true meaning of the term and the humongous difference between just being a body *in* the church, versus a part *of* the body of Christ.

I hope to provoke thought through relevant scriptures and pose meaningful questions to stir your spirit and help you to better fulfill your purpose in life. This manuscript seeks to take on the form of a mirror so that you can really see yourself; it seeks to serve as an internal recorder so that you can hear yourself. It is my desire that you observe the real, unmasked YOU! Afterwards, it is my hope that we can move forward toward becoming all that God expects us to. How can this be done? In my opinion, it is actually a straight-forward process, beginning with the understanding that church folks and Christians are not one in the same; there are some major differences that are recognizable.

3 THERE IS A DIFFERENCE

Understanding the differences between church folks and Christians is not that difficult of a task but it is an essential one. There are some similarities between the two, sure, but ultimately these two concepts are independent of each other. In essence, one of the main differences between the two is that a church person is merely a hearer of the word while a Christian is a doer of the word. James 1:22 says, "But be ye doers of the word, and not hearers only, deceiving your own selves" (KJV). It is not enough to simply sit in the church building on Sundays and Wednesdays, week after week, hearing the word; we have to really listen to the word, absorb it, share it with others, and actually apply it to our daily lives. This sounds like a pretty clear cut, easy task, doesn't it? Well, why do we have such trouble doing it?

The next step involves each person examining him or herself. In 1 Corinthians 11:28, the instructions for each of us are to "let a man examine himself" (KJV). When you complete a detailed examination of yourself, if you are truthful, you will probably be stunned at what the results are. For a few moments, ponder the following questions and the choices that follow:

1. The pastor removes you from a leadership position that you have held for several years; he replaces you with another young lady who has fresh, new ideas and who will do a great job. Do you:

   a. Get angry and stop attending that church

   b. Say nothing, but resentfully continue attending the church, withdrawing your participation from every ministry you once were a part of

   c. Thank the pastor for the opportunity to serve in that capacity and let your replacement know you are willing to help in any way she needs

2. This year the church's anniversary program is to be co-chaired by you and another lady; you have been chair before but it is this lady's first time. Do you:

   a. Basically plan the entire program on your own but let her know that you welcome any of her suggestions

b. Collaborate with her to ensure the program is both pleasing to God and successful

c. Complain to the pastor that she will only get in your way and should be assigned as your assistant

3. You are the Minister of Music and one of the choir members is ill. Do you:

a. Visit him out of sheer concern for his health

b. Send a card and flower because it will look bad if you do not do something nice

c. Not bother doing anything because there are enough choir members sending flowers and visiting him

4. You attend Sunday school regularly and often times participate in reviewing the lesson with your class. Last week, the Assistant Superintendent unintentionally forgot to call your name while he was up thanking your class for reviewing. Do you:

a. Say nothing but make a mental note to watch him to see if he does that again the next time you review

b. Watch each class that reviews weekly to see if he forgets to call anybody else's name

c. Charge that to his mind and not his heart and forget it even happened

5. You are the mother of two small children. One Sunday an usher kindly asks one of your children to take his feet off the seat. Do you:

a. Appreciate the usher for doing her job

b. Get an attitude with the usher for telling your child what to do

c. Go to the usher board president immediately following service to complain

We all know how we should have answered these questions, but we also know how we were realistically responding to ourselves while reading them. We must take honest assessments of how we treat others, the ways we speak, the thoughts we think, and the ways we carry ourselves. Do we always respond in ways that are pleasing to God? Is our conduct similar to that of Christ when He walked this earth for those thirty-three years? Do our mindsets, behaviors, and conversations resemble that of Jesus Christ *at least* the majority of the time? It would be ideal if we, day in and day out, consistently bear a resemblance to Christ; however, because the flesh is weak, this is not always the case. It is imperative that we always make an effort to resemble Christ in everything we do and say. Philippians 2:5 says, "Let this mind be in you, which was also in Christ Jesus" (KJV). Your attitude should be the same as that of Jesus Christ- day in and day out. If you cannot truly say that your attitude mirrors that of Christ more times than not, then, most likely, you are not living up to the real meaning of the word, "Christian."

By now, have you figured out that half-stepping on this journey, mistreating others, and living any old kind of way will not secure you a place in Heaven? Have you figured out that God can see right through counterfeit church people? Running all around the church, shouting harder and louder than everyone else, gets you nowhere with God. You do know that God is not interested in fake acts of adoration and phony praise, right? He has beautiful angels singing His praises and magnifying His name, so we should understand that we are not needed by God. Honestly, it is a privilege that God created us and allows us to serve Him, so we should be completely honored by this.

We were formed to praise God, to glorify Him, to love one another, and be disciples for Him. Think about this for a minute: how is being fake and phony, and not doing what God commands of us, beneficial to us? How does criticizing others and quarreling in the church, which, of course, discourages people from coming to church, fulfill the purpose for which we were created? These things do not fulfill our purposes or profit us at all; yet, we still entertain this foolishness. Isn't it good to know that it is never too late to change and stop dabbling in silliness?

Internally, we must decide to do and be better! This begins with making up one's mind to make changes and being open-minded enough to see things from different perspectives. Prayerfully, journeying through this book will assist in making that happen. It is my hope that the scriptures that are presented throughout the text grab hold to your thoughts, causing you to examine your current spiritual state; you may not be aware of certain weaknesses you may have. I definitely was not aware of some of the frightening characteristics I possessed and, as I pointed out earlier, I am still recognizing areas of needed improvement. After all, this Christian journey is on-going, so one will never stop learning and needing to do better.

Below is a list, not completely exhaustive, of some common characteristics of church folks. Typical church folks:

- Put self first instead of last

- Operate in responsibility not love

- Look at Christianity as a temporary situation instead of a lifestyle

- Are hypocritical and fake, not genuine and sincere

- Are disruptive instead of harmonious

- Are too busy with church programs to fulfill purpose

- Are more concerned with positions than praise

- Are more excited about titles than testimonies

- Are concerned with personal recognition instead of God's righteousness

- Are normally critics instead of encouragers

- Are busy yet not productive

- Are haughty and proud instead of humble and lowly

- Are "moved" only when they have a role in the "moving."

- See the wrong in others but not in self

- Take the phrase "God knows my heart" lightly

- Make excuses instead of improvements

- Misconstrue the meaning of the phrase "Come as you are"

- Do not know when to be quiet

- Can quote scriptures but do not demonstrate them

- Promote condemnation instead of restoration

- Profess to love God but do not intimately know Him

Many of these attributes will be addressed throughout this book; unfortunately, all too often, we can take credit for displaying these. Do any of these look familiar to you; are you guilty of possessing any of these traits? If so, are you willing to change that?

4 THAT LITTLE TONGUE

It is a known fact that the human body is a complex system made up of many cells, bones, muscles and organs. If you have ever studied the human body then you may know just how complex it is. It is said that an adult body is made up of one hundred trillion cells, two hundred and six bones, six hundred muscles, and twenty-two internal organs. Each of these components of the human body is essential, mandatory, and should be handled with care; but of the twenty-two internal organs, there is one in particular that requires special care. Which organ is it? I am so glad you asked; it is the untamable tongue! There are tons of famous quotes about the dangers of not using the tongue properly, the power that lies within the tongue, and how the tongue can increase your credibility or discount it; likewise, the Bible makes many references to the tongue as well.

Robert Frost once said, "Half the world is composed of people who have something to say and cannot, and the other half who have nothing to say and keep on saying it." On this same note George Eliot says, "Blessed is the man who, having nothing to say, abstains from giving wordy evidence of that fact." There are so many of us who obviously have never heard these quotes before; we fit the bill too well to be aware of them. Some of us really like to hear ourselves talk, don't we? We can really say a lot of different "stuff" too.

    This holds true whether we are actually experts on the topic or not. Some of us truly seem to think we actually know something about everything! Regardless of the topic, and whatever the issue, we seem to readily have a remedy, solution, or some type of unsolicited advice to offer. Why do you think this is? Is it because we have low self-esteem and have to build ourselves up by sounding intelligent or knowledgeable? Do we actually believe we are saying something of importance when we are babbling? Well, there is an Italian proverb that states, "He who knows little knows enough if he knows how to hold his tongue." This quote says a lot; if a person knows when to hold his or her tongue, then this person knows plenty!

    We, as individuals, have to learn that we cannot talk all of the time; if we do, we are going to miss out on something. An American proverb represents this point by indicating that we should, "Listen or thy tongue will keep thee deaf." It is amazing how true these quotes are! Our tongues can truly limit us from hearing vital information, whether from God, our pastors, family members, or even our bosses. There have been occurrences when I personally have been waiting on an answer from God and, after a certain amount of time had elapsed, asked myself if I had missed hearing His answer because I was talking so much. I have heard of instances in which something bad happened, like a person's child committed suicide, or a person was laid off from a job; because they did not take the time to listen, they missed the warnings the child or supervisor had given. This is unfortunate! To ensure no misfortunes like these happen in the future, we should observe the Turkish proverb that says, "Having two ears and one tongue, we should listen twice as much as we speak." Similarly, James 1:19 instructs every man to be "swift to hear, slow to speak, and slow to wrath" (KJV). Have you noticed that we do the complete opposite?

When we were younger my sister and I would be excited when our mother returned from the grocery store because we knew she bought snacks for us. We would attempt to overindulge ourselves by eating up the snacks all at once. Mom would say, "Just because you know the snacks are in there does not mean you have to eat them all up tonight; they are not going anywhere." This holds true for our tongues; just because we know we have one does not mean we have to use it all of the time or all at once; it is not going anywhere. The point I am making is that silence is just as golden as your words; one has to know when to speak and when to be quiet.

Silence is not always looked at the way it should be. Often times, silence is looked at as a sign of being guilty, incompetent, or stupid. I am here to remind you that silence does not always have to be bad; it does not only indicate these downbeat factors. In some cases, silence indicates just the opposite. Instead of always being seen in a negative light, silence should sometimes be viewed positively. One positive way silence can be viewed is as an indication of wisdom. If correctly executed, being silent can demonstrate how wise a person is; in fact, Shakespeare said "Men of few words are the best men." Also, there is a traditional proverb that states, "A still tongue makes a wise head." Being silent is not a bad thing and does not mean that one has nothing to say; it signifies that one is wise enough to know *when* to have something to say.

Secondly, silence is valuable. One Hebrew proverb says, "If a word is worth one shekel, silence is worth two." During a period of silence, one can actually hear; this sounds so simple yet, often times, we miss this modest point. Matthew 11:15 declares "Whoever has ears, let them hear" (NIV). Silence is worth much when one is listening to hear worthwhile information; of course, any information from God is worthwhile. To illustrate this fact, Job 29:21 says, "Men listened to me expectantly, waiting in silence for my counsel" (NIV). It is obvious here that Job had valuable information to relay; the fact that men waited patiently around him to hear his guidance proves this point. Of course, Job had valuable counsel because he was wise enough to seek God. Although I wasn't around, I am sure that Job spent much time listening to God. It definitely pays to be silent; in silence one is able to hear instruction from the Almighty.

Finally, silence is powerful. Phillips Brooks affirms, "A man who lives right, and is right, has more power in his silence than another has by his words." Simply put, if one lives and is right, there is really nothing that needs to be said; this person's silence is more powerful than his or her words because his or her actions speak louder than words. To further drive this point, the sixth chapter of Joshua demonstrates how powerful silence can be; in some cases, there is victory and triumph in silence. In this chapter, God gives the victory to Joshua and His people. Per God's instructions, Joshua 6:10 relays, "And Joshua had commanded the people, saying, you shall not shout, nor make any noise with your voice, neither shall any word proceed out of your mouth until the day I bid you shout; then shall you shout" (AKJV). The people and Joshua did as God commanded and, ultimately, the victory belonged to them. As evident here, silence can lead to victory. So, now that we are familiar with the benefits of being quiet, let us begin to exercise one of our God-given rights: we have the right to remain silent!

There is so much that can be said about the tongue; it has so many traits: it is useful, dangerous, wild, small, and powerful just to name a few. If you attend church even occasionally, most likely you have heard a portion of Proverbs 18:21 that states, "Death and life are in the power of the tongue" (KJV). Even though I have heard this scripture quoted innumerable times, I am just now starting to realize how influential this is. Do you realize that through God, we, using our mouths to form words, can completely turn a situation around and make it work out in our favor? At the same time, without God, we, still using our mouths to form words, can completely negate a situation as well. Basically, in the fourth chapter of Romans, we are informed that we are to call those things which are not as though they are. Do you know what this means? Your tongue, through faith in God, can work situations out for your good! In fact, Romans 8:28 states, "And we know that all things work together for good to them that love God, to them who are the called according to His purpose" (KJV).

The scriptures above relay a very important message: the tongue, though small, can do big things-REALLY big things! James 3:5 tells us, "Even so the tongue is a little member, and boasteth great things" (KJV). Aside from amazingly speaking life or death over a situation, the tongue can build up a person's character or restore someone's self-esteem. There are lots of triumphant stories about individuals who were once on the brink of suicide but had someone, a counselor, a friend, or a favorite relative, speak kind words to them to encourage them to change their minds. There are other instances where successful scholars who, at one point were underachievers, had educators in their corners to motivate them to strive for excellence and become great. The tongue can put a smile on a sad face or give joy to a discontented spirit; it can be a tool of encouragement and motivation.

On the flip side, it must be noted that the tongue can also be a huge source of discouragement; it can turn a cheerful smile into a disheartened frown. It is so influential that it can tear apart families, tear down churches, break an individual's heart, or even provoke someone to take his or her own life. Sadly, there are many stories about individuals who, already low in self-esteem, take their own lives as a result of someone else's words. Bullying, which can be physical or mental, has become a huge problem in today's society; many cases of bullying are caused simply by the misuse of the tongue. This little fleshy organ inside the mouth can bring about some awesome or awful results; it all depends on how it is used. Basically, the tongue can harm others, the church, or your own self if you are not careful.

In chapter three of the book of James, the writer says that just as a small fire can destroy an entire forest, so can the tiny tongue taint the entire body. Whoa! Remember, the body is comprised of one hundred trillion cells, two hundred and six bones, six hundred muscles, and twenty-two internal organs. Do we really believe the tiny tongue can do that much damage? We need to believe it!

James continues on saying that every kind of beast, birds, and serpents is tamed, "But the tongue can no man tame; it is an unruly evil, full of deadly poison" (James 3:7-8, KJV). It is amazing how much damage or impairing the tongue can do!

From birth, throughout our teenage years, and on into adulthood, we are taught that our mouths can get us into trouble, cause trouble for others, or even prevent trouble. I am positive that you can think back to a time where your mouth either helped you avoid getting into trouble with your parents, or caused you to get into trouble with your teacher. Another time your mouth possibly helped you get a promotion or avoid termination on your job. Maybe you can remember an instance when your mouth soothed someone's aching heart or troubled someone's confused mind. At any rate, I cannot stress enough the importance of using the tongue wisely.

The Bible, time and time again, stresses the importance of utilizing the tongue properly; we are warned about speaking good things and watching what we say. Psalm 34:13 instructs us to "Keep thy tongue from evil, and thy lips from speaking guile" (KJV). 1 Peter 3:10 restates, "For he that will love life, and see good days, let him refrain his tongue from evil, and his lips that they speak no guile" (KJV). In plain terms, we are to not speak evil and devious things; by refraining from such deviousness, we will see good days. Proverbs 15:4 tells us that, "A wholesome tongue is a tree of life, but perverseness therein is a breach in the spirit" (KJV). In this scripture, a wholesome tongue is a hearty, healthy tongue that is compared to a tree of life; however, a tongue that speaks unreasonableness is a violation in the spirit. This is dangerous territory for we know how important the spirit is. Our Father, God, is a spirit; the Bible explicitly states this. It goes on to tell us how significant the spirit is. Romans 8:6 says, "For to be carnally minded is death, but to be spiritually minded is life and peace" (KJV). The spirit is very important I tell you; these scriptures illustrate how vital the spirit is, thus, in turn, demonstrate just how important it is to use the tongue positively.

In James 1:26, we are told that, "If any man among you seem to be religious, and bridleth not his tongue, but deceiveth his own heart, this man's religion is vain" (KJV). In other words, if an individual seems to be religious by walking and talking like he or she is saved, however, does not exercise restraint or control of the tongue, this person deceives him or her own self. Case in point: The church's usher board president knows the Bible, can pray well, and is considered to be a classy lady. The problem with this church person is that she verbally murders other females for how they dress or wear their hair. She hates when they wear pants because she feels women are supposed to wear dresses; she hates the dresses they wear because they are too casual-looking for church. She complains about the hairstyles the women of the church wear; the color is too loud or the styles make them look too young for their ages. Whatever she thinks about these women and their attire comes out of her mouth. She walks around looking like a saint, but cannot or will not control the words that come out of her mouth.

Another case in point: the chairman of the deacon board smiles and greets everyone that enters into the doors of the church building. He voluntarily unlocks the church doors and gets the air or heat generating in preparation for all programs and rehearsals. He works hard and contributes a lot to the upkeep and maintenance of the edifice. Great! However, his downfall is that he continuously criticizes the other deacons for not doing all that he does; he is quick to harshly voice his disapproval about their lax attitudes regarding church business. According to scripture, the religion of the usher board president and deacon is ineffective and worthless. I reiterate that, according to scripture, if individuals around you appear to be religious, but cannot control their mouths, then they deceive themselves by thinking that their religion is of any worth. That's deep. Why would you want your religion to mean nothing to God or to any other Christian for that matter? What am I saying? I am saying that our labor, dedication, and contribution to the church could be null and void because of our tongues.

We, as Christians, cannot say anything we want or blurt out whatever we are thinking when we feel like it. There is another famous quote about the tongue by Iara Gassen; it says, "Be careful of your thoughts; they may become words." This holds especially true if what we are thinking is ungodly; we are to restrain from ungodliness and retain our tongues for good use. James 3:9 points out, "With the tongue we praise our Lord and Father, and with it we curse human beings, who have been made in God's likeness" (NIV). This is so sad but true. One second a praise for our Father is resting on our lips; the next second a curse is stumbling out of our mouths. Out of the same mouth should not come praising and cursing; this just should not be and we know it. Undoubtedly, our conversation is supposed to consist of things that Christ would say. If it does not, we could end up doing some serious damage with our little tongues. Just as David proclaims in the thirty-ninth chapter of Psalm, so should we affirm "I will take heed to my ways, that I sin not with my tongue" (Psalm 39:1, KJV).

Things we say can seriously hurt other people. Yes, I remember the old idiom that states, "Sticks and stones may break my bones, but words will never hurt me." My parents taught this popular phrase to my siblings and me. To an extent, it is true; in fact, I introduced it to my oldest daughter in a discussion about self-esteem. This phrase is great to hold on to when dealing with certain worldly issues. It sometimes remedies the situation or at least makes us feel better when we think about it. However, regarding the Christian world, there should be no need to have to use this phrase because, ideally, in God's house, hateful, harmful words should not exist, but they do. This is ill-fated because Matthew 12:36-37 warns us that, "for every idle word men may speak, they will give account of it in the day of judgment; for by your words you will be justified, and by your words you will be condemned" (NKJV). We seem to think it is okay to use our tongues in any way we choose; this is not acceptable and we will be held accountable.

Those who profess Jesus as their personal Savior should never utilize their tongues to do harm; detrimental words can ultimately destroy another person. In extreme cases our tongues can turn someone seeking after God completely away from God. We must definitely avoid this terrible act; we are to be diplomats for Christ. 2 Corinthians 5:20 tells us, "Now then we are ambassadors for Christ" (KJV). This means everything we say is to represent Christ so that we can draw the unsaved to God. Jesus states in John 14:6, "I am the way, the truth, and the life: no man cometh unto the Father, but by me" (KJV). When we speak in ways that do not represent Jesus' speech, we stand the risk of hindering some man or woman from getting to God because he or she will be turned off by Jesus' "so-called" ambassadors.

Here is a great illustration: a young lady, with two small children and no wedding ring on her finger comes to church. She has on slacks, a spaghetti strapped shirt, and some four-inch stiletto sandals. She arrives late, during prayer time, walking through a door that does not have an usher on post. She is stopped abruptly and, immediately following the prayer, is insensitively scolded for walking at an inappropriate time; on top of that, she is reprimanded for the outfit she has on. All of this happens in front of the children and the other spectators who are staring her up and down from head to toe. The lady is now embarrassed, angry, and, of course, does not want to spend another second among those people. Okay…let us evaluate the situation; it is right to stop the lady from walking during prayer and even acceptable to discuss her choice of clothing with her. It is not right for anyone to form negative assumptions about the woman (I am confident that many of you readers also started forming opinions of her in your mind immediately upon reading the scenario too) or talk to the woman insensitively in front of her children or any other person. For all we know, this lady could have not been brought up in the church; therefore, she would not know "church etiquette." Also, she may have worn all that she had to wear to church that morning. What we do know is that because of the unsympathetic way the church folks treated her, she may never return to that church, or any other, again!

This is what we do not want to happen, yet it does. If we are to draw people into the church, we cannot let our preconceived notions, prejudices, or knowledge of church etiquette push them away from the church. We surely cannot let our words or the way in which we say our words discourage a person from visiting God's house. If we say we are Christians, guess what? We cannot be guilty of turning others away; we are to be disciples of Jesus Christ. John 8:31 says, "If ye continue in my word, then are ye my disciples indeed" (KJV). Abiding in His word means the whole word, not half of it; we cannot abide by the bits and pieces that sound good to us. Also, abiding in the word means adhering to the scriptures that warn us of how we are to control, restrain, and utilize the tongue. As disciples, we are to embrace every person, particularly the sinner. We are to rebuke the sin, yet love the sinner and help him or her repent of his or her sinful nature; we cannot do this by speaking roughly or thoughtlessly. Nobody likes to be talked to any kind of way- including you.

The key to properly handling the tongue is to speak kindly and decently, and to do it in love. Please keep in mind the words of Robert Burton who said, "A blow with a word strikes deeper than a blow with a sword." Once a hurtful word leaves your lips, it cannot return. Just like a knife, hurtful words cut deeply and the wounds are slow to heal. Church folks need to understand this fact; even more importantly, we should take Proverbs 12:18 to heart. This scripture states, "The words of the reckless pierce like swords, but the tongue of the wise brings healing" (NIV). Let us not continue speaking recklessly and ignorantly because it is not of God and definitely is not Christian-like. Consider Proverbs 21:23 which asserts, "Those who guard their mouths and their tongues keep themselves from calamity" (NIV). Keeping your mouth closed, or at least thinking before speaking, will keep you clear of mishaps. In fact, many of the fall-outs that occur among church members are a result of someone saying too much or saying the wrong thing in the wrong way. This can be changed beginning with that little tongue!

5 SO BUSY

Busy is a word we hear a lot these days. There are different ways, both positive and negative, that a person can be busy. Being busy can involve being meddlesome or intrusive; this can be a huge interference in God's business. Also, being busy means being physically engaged in acts or thought; this can be a good thing or a bad thing, depending on how busy you are and what you are busy doing or thinking. The devil likes for Christians to be busy; if we stay physically busy, overwhelmed with daily life, we cannot be spiritually busy working on the battlefield for the Lord.

On the flip side, being busy can involve being proactive, hands-on, or diligent. This is the form of being busy that really counts; it is very necessary because there is much work for a Christian to do. In chapter nine of the book of Matthew, in verses 37 and 38, it is stated, "Then He said to his disciples, the harvest is plentiful but the workers are few; ask the Lord of the harvest, therefore, to send out workers into his harvest field" (NIV). All Jesus is saying here is that there is much work to do, yet there are few who are really willing, able, and prepared to work. This is bewildering because we, Christians, are supposed to be willing servants; we are to always have a desire to be used by God to help others and fulfill His purpose.

Increasingly, more and more people are getting busy making sure those around them are aware of just how busy they are; this is so funny to me. A close friend of mine and I often times discuss the fact that truly busy people do not have the time to talk about how busy they are; she and I always ask, "Who does that?" A really busy person couldn't! If you have time to parade around declaring your busyness, then when do you have time to complete the work that causes you to be so busy? Also, what are you busy accomplishing and who are you working for? You may want to stop and assess who it is employing you and determine who is getting the glory. It may just be that you are busy working to better yourself, provide for your family, achieve fame, or attain fortune, or you could be unknowingly on an assignment for the devil himself. Regardless of what or who you are working for, if it is not for the glory of God, it means nothing. Below is a piece, written by Dale Hill of Dale Hill Ministries, about being busy; he really hits the nail on the head! Dale Hill's work is entitled *Satan's Meeting* and is as follows:

Satan called a worldwide convention of

demons. In his opening address he said, "We can't keep Christians from going to church. We can't keep them from reading their Bibles and knowing the truth. We can't even keep them from forming an intimate relationship with their Savior. Once they gain that connection with Jesus, our power over them is broken. So let them go to their churches; let them have their covered dish dinners, BUT steal their time, so they don't have time to develop a relationship with Jesus Christ." The devil continued, "This is what I want you to do: Distract them from gaining hold of their Savior and maintaining that vital connection throughout their day!" "How shall we do this" his demons shouted. "Keep them busy in the non-essentials of life and invent innumerable schemes to occupy their minds," he answered. "Tempt them to spend, spend, spend, and borrow, borrow, borrow. Persuade the wives to go to work for long hours and the husbands to work 6-7 days each week, 10-12 hours a day, so they can afford their empty lifestyles. Keep them from spending time with their children. As their families fragment, soon, their homes will offer no escape from the pressures of work! Over-stimulate their minds so that they cannot hear that still, small voice. Entice them to play the radio or cassette player whenever they drive; to keep the TV, VCR, CDs and their PCs going constantly in their home and see to it that every store and restaurant in the world plays non-biblical music constantly. This will jam their minds and break that union with Christ. Fill the coffee tables with magazines and newspapers. Pound their minds with the news 24 hours a day. Invade their driving moments with billboards. Flood their mailboxes with junk mail, mail order catalogs, sweepstakes, and every kind of newsletter and promotional offering free products, services, and false hopes. Keep skinny, beautiful models on the magazines and TV so their husbands will believe that outward beauty is what's important, and they'll become dissatisfied with their wives. Keep the wives too tired to love their husbands at night. Give them headaches, too! If they don't give their husbands the love they need, they will begin to look elsewhere. That will fragment their families quickly! Give them Santa Claus to distract them from teaching their children the real meaning of Christmas. Give them an Easter bunny so they won't talk about his resurrection and power over sin and death. Even in their recreation, let them be excessive. Have them return from their recreation exhausted. Keep them too busy to go out in nature and reflect on God's creation. Send them to amusement parks, sporting events, plays, concerts, and movies instead. Keep them busy, busy, busy! And when they meet for spiritual fellowship, involve them in gossip and small talk so that they leave with troubled consciences. Crowd their lives with so many good causes they have no time to seek power from Jesus. Soon they will be working in their own strength, sacrificing their health and family for the good of the cause. It will work! It will work! "It was quite a plan! The demons went eagerly to their assignments, causing Christians everywhere to get busier and more rushed, going here and there, having little time for their God or their families; having no time to tell others about the power of Jesus to change lives. I guess the question is, has the devil been successful in his schemes? You be the judge!!!!!

At the conclusion of the work, Dale Hill asks, "Does being busy mean being under Satan's yoke?" We should really think about this.

In addition to the fact that the devil wants us to be busy so that he can try to shift our focus from God to worldly or ungodly things, God wants us to be busy too-enhancing the kingdom. Nevertheless, we must be careful of how we approach being busy and we must not be too busy that we miss out on what God has for us. You probably recall the story of Mary and Martha. In this story, which is found in the tenth chapter of Luke, we find out that Jesus was coming to visit the two sisters. All day

Martha busily cleaned and cooked, preparing for Jesus' arrival. Once Jesus did arrive, she continued making preparations to ensure Jesus was comfortable. After a while, Martha, still busy playing the host, got agitated with her sister because, in her eyes, Mary was doing nothing. Upon complaining to Jesus about how wrong Mary was for not assisting her, Martha was corrected; Jesus told her that Mary was doing just what she was supposed to be doing- being busy visiting with Him while she (Martha) was too busy with the inessentials, thus missing out on an opportunity to fellowship with Him.

One formal definition of busy, according to Merriam-Webster online, is engaged in action or being in use. This source also states that being busy could mean foolishly or intrusively active, which easily transforms into meddling. Now you may recall that my list from chapter three indicated church folks are busy, yet not productive. What is the difference you may ask? There are several differences between being busy and being productive.

According to Merriam-Webster online, the term productive has various definitions, but the first three are of use in this case. The first definition of productive is having the quality or power of producing, especially in abundance.

The second definition says being productive is effective in bringing about results. Finally, the third definition states that being productive is yielding results, benefits, or profits. This definition is my personal favorite because it best describes what it is to be a Christian. To be a true Christian, as I am going to repeat throughout this text, is to be just as Christ; yielding results. As recorded in the Bible, nothing that Jesus did- and He did an abundance of things- failed to yield a result. Not only did Jesus yield results, these results were benefits that we profited from. Jesus, in obedience to our Father, brought about results in the Bible days and He did so in abundance. He still operates that way, on our behalf, today.

Just think about this...everything Jesus did was done as a benefit to us. He lived for us, died for us, and rose for us. You know all of this, right? Of course you do; however, humor me for just a little while. Jesus' life was purposed to save our lives; this is why He was ever born of Mary. Jesus *taught* so that we will know the truth, He *healed* so that we will know the power of the Almighty, and He *lived* to serve as a fleshly example of righteousness. His life was the ultimate model for us to follow daily so that we can live virtuous lifestyles and be holy in the sight of God.

All of this illustrates the point I am trying to make: Christians are to live productive, useful lives, not busy lives.

In exploration of the term productive, it must be thoroughly understood that Christians are not to be productive simply for "self." Productivity, from a Christian's standpoint, should be for the benefit or gain of others, particularly the unsaved. The work and good deeds Christians do should not solely be for self; this goes against what the Word says. In many instances, the Bible teaches that selfishness is not of God; this will be explored in-depth in the next chapter. All that should be made known for the time being is that the results Christians are to yield are to be profited by others. In order to bring about results, however, we cannot behave as mere church folks, busy meddling and talking about how busy we are, but as Christians who are realistically working to yield positive outcomes.

At the church that you attend or visit, are there any programs that you can think of that occur annually? These programs are normally the big fundraisers for the church; the proceeds generally go to the church's building fund, the youth or music department's treasury, or, to the pastor as a token of appreciation. In many of the churches that I know of, there are several huge annual programs and events which allow the busiest and hardest-working saints in the church an opportunity to shine. They shine because their names are printed on the programs, they get the opportunity to delegate tasks to others, and they get the chance to flaunt their new outfits and shoes because they sit on the front row or walk up and down the aisle, back and forth, throughout the program. This allows the congregation to see them. Examples of these programs are: church anniversaries, pastor anniversaries, Vacation Bible school, choir anniversaries, Men's Day, and Women in Red, just to name a few. I am sure you are smiling to yourself because you know exactly what I am talking about and have experienced people like this at some of these programs.

For some reason, there is, often times, a lot of bickering and falling out among the committee members leading up to the day of the event. There are normally two or three chiefs and no Indians; in some cases, there seems to be small turnouts because the majority of the church does not even want to attend the program due to all of the squabbling that takes place leading up to the day of the program. Why is this? We all know why. There are always certain individuals who have to have their names called; they madly, to no avail, work, constantly complaining about how hard they work and how unappreciated they feel, how they don't have any help, and how the pastor always assigns them the task. "Their event" must be a success; after all, there will be guests in attendance and everything has to work perfectly. The church has got to look good, right? Wrong! They, these "saints," have to look good! What these church folks do not admit is how badly they want to hear their names called, how they honestly do not want any help-because then they would have to share some of their spotlight, and how they ask the pastor year after year if they can chair the event again. All of this for self; no one is profiting but the individual getting the praise.

Other than the definitions previously discussed, what else do we know about being busy? One source states that a busybody is one who meddles or pries into the affairs of others. This person is a meddlesome, prying, or officious person. What exactly does this mean? An officious person is marked by excessive eagerness in offering unwanted services or advice to others. This person unnecessarily is always ready to tell you something about everything whether you ask for the advice or not. Do you know anybody like this? Wait…does this sound like you? Well, if it does, be careful!

In 1 Timothy 5:13 it is stated, "And withal they learn to be idle, wandering about from house to house; and not only idle, but tattlers also and busybodies, speaking things which they ought not" (KJV). In other words, the Bible speaks of individuals who are idle or inoperative; they wander about, gossiping and just being busy doing nothing useful. In this scripture we see that there is nothing beneficial in doing this. Gossip is a sin and being idle is dangerous. I reiterate, in Matthew 12:36, Jesus tells us, "But I say unto you, that every idle word that men shall speak, they shall give account thereof in the Day of Judgment" (KJV). Also, there is a popular English proverb that states "an idle mind is the devil's workshop." You know for yourself that this is true. Whenever we are not occupied with something constructive, our minds get to wandering negatively and we end up doing things that can be destructive. This is precisely why our minds are to be kept on Jesus. Isaiah 26:3 relays to us that God "will keep in perfect peace those whose minds are steadfast" (NIV).

In the twenty-second chapter of Proverbs, it is stated that a man diligent in his own business shall stand before kings. Ponder this for a second. We, if we are diligent in our business of kingdom building, and not being foolish, can stand before the King of Kings. This should be incentive enough for us to work hard on yielding positive, useful results instead of shooting off at the mouth about how much work we are doing around the church and in our lives; this is just hot air. Only we, ourselves, care about how busy we claim to be; God certainly does not have a want or need to hear about it. Besides, there is not one instance that I know of in the Bible where Jesus bragged to His disciples about how busy He was, how many souls He saved, how many miracles He performed, or how important He is to the kingdom. So, how about following Jesus' example by focusing on demonstrating productivity instead of being a busybody?

6 THE "I" IN "CHURCH"

Spelling has never been a big problem for me. Of course, I am not claiming to be the best speller in the world but, for the most part, I spell pretty well. Because of this, I can confidently say that the word "church" does not have an "I" in it. However, when looking at many churches today, you would never know that. This is because we have become so caught up in what we want, not what God or our fellow man wants.

Dr. Martin Luther King, Jr. once said, "Every man must decide whether he will walk in the light of creative altruism or in the darkness of destructive selfishness." Altruism is synonymous to selflessness. So, in essence, Dr. King is saying each of us must choose if we want to walk in light, which is selflessness, or in darkness, which is selfishness. When it comes to church, there should be no question as to which route we will choose. Guess what? In certain churches, it is unfortunate, yet obvious, that the path of selflessness is not even an option.

The concept of selfishness is not new; it has always been around, but it seems to be growing in popularity day by day. This is very unfortunate because being selfish only benefits self, stirs up hatred, and sometimes violence, and even leads to death in extreme cases. The concept of selfishness is not to be taken lightly, nor should it be easily dismissed. It should be worked on. According to William E. Gladstone, "Selfishness is the greatest curse of the human race." We know that curses are evil, mean, and sometimes are sources of harm. Being selfish is very risky.

Selfishness starts in various ways. In many cases, it stems from those who think very highly of themselves. Thinking highly of self is good, to a certain degree, because it signifies good self-esteem within. Having high self-esteem and self-confidence is useful as well as gratifying. However, if one begins thinking too highly of him or herself, this could lead to conceitedness, which could give way to selfish acts. This is part of the problem with today's society; as a whole, we are selfish. We are so selfish that we cut people off on the road when we are in a hurry. We cut others off while they are talking when we feel we have something more important to say. We disregard certain rules and regulations when we feel the need. Selfish individuals steal from others or pay no mind to hurting other people's feelings. The list goes on and on.

Another thing selfishness does is give rise to the crab

mentality. You have heard of the crab mentality, right? This concept is derived from a story about a bucket of crabs. There are different variations; however, the moral of the story is the same. According to one version of the story, a man decides to grab a bucket and go out in search of fresh crabs one day. Not long after he sets out, he is able to capture one live crab. He grabs his bucket & places the crab inside. A short while later the man glances down in his bucket only to realize that the crab had escaped. Upset with himself for forgetting to bring the lid to the bucket, the man starts searching again for crabs. As luck would have it, the man comes across six more crabs on his way back home. When he reaches his destination, to his astonishment, all six crabs are still there. This puzzles the man, so he decides to observe the crabs for a while. After watching the crabs interact, the owner realizes the mentality of the crab. Basically, this mentality is best relayed by the statement, "If I can't have it, neither should you." The owner realized that if each crab was in its own bucket, each would have easily escaped. Because the six crabs were in the bucket together, and neither wanted the other to escape, all crabs remained trapped. If one crab started making progress toward freedom, the other crabs would pull it down. Due to selfishness, every crab in the bucket faced the same ill fate in the end.

In the world, we hear stories like this all of the time. There are so many people who possess the crab mentality. Some women shoot their ex-boyfriends' new girlfriends because of this mindset. Estranged husbands kill their ex-wives because of this outlook. Co-workers sabotage the possible career growth of other co-workers as a result of this twisted attitude. Now, here's the kicker-not only in the world is this happening, but this irrational mentality is running wild in the church also. There are certain people in the church who feel like if they can't get elected to a particular position or be given a specific title, then nobody needs to hold the position or title. Others think if they are not blessed with a certain gift, nobody else should have been blessed with it. Basically, this attitude is only good for holding others back from attaining their goals. This is contrary to what God expects and what Jesus demonstrated.

Holding others back conflicts with God's expectations of us. We are to always lend a helping hand and do whatever is necessary to help others to move forward. Not only that, we should also show concern for somebody else other than ourselves. As we should already know, we are to look out for the interests of others. This is not something that just shows that we are good people, but obedient children of the Most High. We are to not dwell solely on our personal needs, cares, and wants. More importantly, we are to focus on the interests of Christ. What interests are these you may wonder? Jesus cares about how we treat our neighbors, our enemies, and our church family members. Mainly, His interests consist of us keeping the commandments of God and living acceptable lives, patterning our lifestyles after His.

Philippians 2:21 says, "For everyone looks out for their own interests, not those of Jesus Christ" (NIV). "I," "my," and "mine" seems to be much of what our conversations are about; seemingly, this is all we care about. Our interests tend to take precedence over everything and everybody; this includes the interests of Jesus Christ! Spiritually speaking, how backwards is that? The love of God is not visible when our needs trample over the needs of others; it definitely is not evident when we have an abundance of resources and possessions and won't share with those in need. Multiple scriptures discuss this concept; some scriptures dwell more on material possessions, while others dwell on more spiritual aspects.

One scripture that makes mention of tangible possessions is 1 John 3:17, which states, "If anyone has material possessions and sees a brother or sister in need but has no pity on them, how can the love of God be in that person" (NIV)? Not only does this concept of selflessness apply physically, but it applies spiritually and emotionally also. If a brother or sister in Christ is in need spiritually, emotionally, or financially, if at all possible, we are to cater to that need. If someone outside of Christ is in need, no matter what the need, if we possess the appropriate resources, we are to place this necessity above our own. In order to this, we have to stop making everything about us.

How can we stop thinking, "It's all about me?" For one, don't be vain, conceited, and haughty. These are ungodly characteristics that are biblically rebuked. Philippians 2:3 instructs us to "Do nothing out of selfish ambition or vain conceit. Rather, in humility value others above yourselves" (NIV). So, in other words, we must stop thinking that we, as individuals, are the top dog, all that, and the most important person in the world. We are to be lowly and humble, like Jesus was, and value our neighbors, friends, church members, and enemies above ourselves. Verse four of this same text continues, "Not looking to your own interests but each of you to the interests of others" (NIV). Similarly, 1 Corinthians 10:24 tells us, "No one should seek their own good, but the good of others" (NIV). Just to be clear, we are to consider the needs of others; in return, God will see to our needs. This, in itself, should be enough comfort for us to work on eliminating our selfish ways.

Writer Oscar Wilde said, "Selfishness is not living as one wishes to live, it is asking others to live as one wishes to live." This is a precise and polite definition of what selfishness is. We cannot expect others to do what we want, say what we want, and act the way we want just because we want them to. Who are we supposed to be? What gives us the right to even think things should always go our way or that we should always have what we want? Seriously, it is imperative for us to learn that everything cannot and will not be about us.

Ironically, we make everything about us, somehow, even in the church. We manage to make programs, positions, and ministries all about us. Initially, the ministry starts off being about God; a short time later, the ministry has become "my ministry." At the start, the committee is all about making the church attractive to outsiders; now, the committee belongs to you and is all about making you look good. The last time I checked, everything we do in this life, especially with regard to the operation of the church, is supposed to be about God. From my understanding, Christians are to be promoting and demonstrating the teachings of Jesus Christ, not of ourselves. Why then is Christ barely visible in many of the events, efforts, and actions we take part in? It is almost as if He has no place in these things.

There is an admirable quote by Cesare Parese which states, "If you wish to travel far and fast, travel light; take off all your envies, jealousies, selfishness, and fears." This is so true; by shedding these unfavorable qualities, you are sure to get further in life faster. With respect to Christians, the attributes above are not even of God and will only hold us back as we journey forward and upward. We will not see heaven by continuing to travel with this kind of baggage. Also, there is no way we can achieve anything great being weighed down with such nonsense. A wonderful quote by Napoleon Hill relays, "Great achievement is usually born of great sacrifice, and is never the result of selfishness." This quote speaks volumes, so let the church say, "Amen."

Before I bring this chapter to a close, I must make mention

of a beautiful song by William McDowell that took the gospel world by storm a short time ago. The chorus of the song quietly relays, "I give myself away so you can use me." In his verse, he sings, "Here I am, here I stand; Lord, my life is in your hands. Lord, I'm longing to see your desires revealed in me; I give myself away." As if this isn't enough, the song goes on to say, "Take my heart; take my life, as a living sacrifice. All my dreams, all my plans, Lord I place them in your hands." The climax of the song declares, "My life is not my own; to you I belong. I give myself, I give myself to you." How beautiful and selfless is this? Only after we entirely surrender to God, wholly giving ourselves away, will we be able to fully be used by Him.

7 SYNTHETIC SAINT

A few months ago, I was talking to a colleague and friend of mine; she was venting about how fed up she is with self-professed Christians acting any way but as a Christian. She began the conversation by saying, "I am so tired of all of this faking!" She then proceeded to tell me how she was at a choir rehearsal the day before and, while there, she observed a lot of negativity in behavior, body language, and attitude. To sum up the conversation, my friend revealed that she witnessed a lack of respect for the individual in authority, an attitude of disobedience to leadership, and a disregard for the true reason for the rehearsal-to uplift God. She ended by saying that she is sick of folks faking. Needless to say, this was a church choir rehearsal. Wow!

Disrespecting authority figures, disobeying those in leadership, and failing to uplift the glorious name of the Lord is just plain wrong, according to biblical specifications. All throughout the Bible we are taught to obey those in authority, follow leadership, work together in unity, and most importantly, lift up God's holy name. Why then was this antagonistic behavior taking place in a Christian atmosphere? If the truth be told, this negative behavior seems to be the "going thing" in a large number of our churches today. This is a horrid truth. I remember a song recorded by a gospel artist that I had the pleasure of meeting about thirteen years ago. Ms. Angela Spivey's song, entitled, "In the Church," reminds us that lying, jealousy, or any other type of sin should not be in the church. This goes for disregarding or disrespecting people in authority as well as possessing offensive, unpleasant attitudes while in the house of the Lord, or anywhere for that matter. Of course the Bible is filled with information and instructions concerning this. Why then do we, those that are in the church, continue to do those things we are instructed not to do?

Getting back to my friend and our conversation, what made her the angriest was that these same negative attitude-having choir members can shout with the best of them when they are up singing or around other church folks. Our conversation ended with her basically repeating her opening declaration, "I am tired of people faking!" This is not the first time I have heard this, and I am sure you have heard pronouncements like this as well. People outside of the church have stated, on many different occasions, that the fake folks in the church make them sick! This is a horrible thing to hear, especially about those who profess to represent God. So now, what do we do about this? First of all, it is imperative that we take a candid look at ourselves; as stated previously, we need to search within and ask God to remove anything inside of us that is not like Him.

Those outside of the church expect to see something special and unique about those of us in the church. Above all, these people expect to see authenticity, not hypocrisy. Who likes a hypocrite? I am pretty sure you are quickly answering, "I don't!" Before you answer, however, assess yourself. Are you hypocritical? A lot of the time we engage in hypocrisy without even realizing we are doing so. This is why assessing ourselves is so important. David knew this; as a result, his request to God was to, "Create in me a pure heart and renew a steadfast spirit within me" (Psalm 51:10, NIV).

Hypocrisy is not a good concept. The formal definition of hypocrisy, according to Encarta Dictionary, is the false claim to or pretense of having admirable beliefs and principles. Not only that, but, biblically speaking, hypocrisy is frowned upon. In the seventh chapter of Matthew, hypocrisy is discussed with respect to finding fault in others without considering our own fault. In Matthew 23:13, hypocrites are reprimanded. This scripture states, "Woe to you, teachers of the law and Pharisees, you hypocrites! You shut the kingdom of heaven in people's faces. You yourselves do not enter, nor will you let those enter who are trying to" (NIV). Even more frightening, the Bible asserts that hypocrites do not stand a good chance of making it to heaven. In the end, it is revealed that "the angels shall come forth, and sever the wicked from among the just, and shall cast them into the furnace of fire: there shall be wailing and gnashing of teeth" (Matthew 13:49-50, KJV). Tie this scripture in with Matthew 24:51, which states, "He (The Master) will cut him (the wicked servant) to pieces and assign him a place with the hypocrites, where there will be weeping and gnashing of teeth" (NIV). The two scriptures communicate this fact: the wicked and the hypocrites will both be found in hell at the end of the age.

What is so appealing about acting fake? Why do folks put on airs when they are in the presence of certain people or are among other "saints?" Why do people fake like they are upright, perfect Christians? We all know this is not the truth. No one is perfect and, as stated before, God does not expect us to be because we cannot do it.

However, God does expect true worship, real love, and sincere adoration from us. We expect genuine concern and love from Him, and we receive it in every instance. Therefore, He does not deserve anything less.

Because I have been playing piano in the church for many years, I have attended and participated in a lot of different musical programs, choir anniversaries, and other events. From time to time, I have the opportunity to observe the conduct of choir members, directors, soloists, and other musicians during the programs. I like to see how these individuals react to other choirs and groups as they minister. I get so agitated when I see a choir talking, texting, and paying no attention to a group that is up ministering, but wants you to fall out, shout, and dance when it is their turn. I also get bothered when a group or soloist may be paying attention throughout the program, but does not move or gets stirred up for any reason at all, other than during his or her own performance.

Now, I must tell the truth in that everyone is not meant to sing or play an instrument; everyone is not given this gift. Therefore, it is understandable if the reaction to Ms. Average's solo is not the exact same as that of Ms. Songbird's musical rendition. What agitates me would be a scenario like the following: Choir All That has just arrived to a gospel musical. This choir happens to walk in while the spirit is high and the anointing is all over Choir Pure, which is up ministering. Instead of joining in, some of the members of Choir All That begin texting on their phones while others try to "out-sing" the other choir from the pews in the congregation. Still, others sit unstirred and unaffected in any kind of way. However, Choir All That gets called up immediately following Choir Pure. On cue, they begin "performing" with outstretched arms; their facial expressions change, they lift up holy hands, and begin "singing out of their hearts."

I cannot understand this for the life of me! The same choir that sat inattentive and motionless, within minutes, became slain in the spirit. I mean, really? I really cannot see how a true Christian can only "move" when he or she has a role in the "moving." One should not think that the Holy Spirit moves solely when he or she is delivering an expression of praise. What I am saying is that there is no way that a bona fide Christian, who is in the midst of a real worship service or the offering up of true praise, can ignore a move of God simply because he or she is not the one singing, playing, praying, speaking, or preaching. Something is seriously wrong with that!

Another case in point: a church choir director gets temporarily removed from his position. During his short-term demotion, he attends church week after week, sitting lifeless and limp, not moving or participating at all in the music worship service. The same songs that made him dance and jump about in the past did nothing for him during his time-out. The moment he is able to return to directing, he is back to performing and out-dancing the choir members. The songs didn't change, the music didn't change, and the choir's singing didn't worsen. Why then couldn't the choir director "feel" anything during the several weeks that he was not directing? The truth could be that he really did not "feel" anything before; by him not playing a direct role in the worship service, he no longer had an audience to fake for.

Faking in the church does nothing for you. As afore-mentioned, God has no need for deceiving praise and fake acts of adoration from us. Jumping the highest, singing the loudest, praying the longest, preaching the hardest, playing the finest, and leading the best is of no importance to God. He wants sincerity, genuineness, authenticity, and realness. Therefore, taking part in synthetic worship services and offering bogus admiration for Him is a waste of time. We know this because God's word explicitly declares "those who worship Him *must* worship in spirit and in truth." These seem to be words that many church folks have memorized but have not yet made a part of their daily lives. Here, the term "must" is used, indicating that this type of worship is mandatory; therefore, it is in our best interest to follow through with this command.

Specifically, John 4:23-24 captures Jesus' words to a Samaritan woman. In a discussion about where and how worship is to take place, Jesus educates this woman on the sort of worshiper God is looking for. In these scriptures, Jesus declares, "Yet a time is coming and has now come when the true worshipers will worship the Father in spirit and truth, for they are the kind of worshipers the Father seeks" (NIV). Synonyms for the term truth are: actuality, reality, and certainty; antonyms for this term are untruthfulness and dishonesty. Which terms best describe your worship attitude toward Him?

Not only does our worship and praise in the church setting need to be real, our daily lives have to be real also. All of our actions have to line up with our speech, mentality, and behavior. If we are not careful and these things don't match up, we could end up doing some extreme damage. People are watching us, so we have to be careful how we live, speak, and act. We cannot quote scriptures and belt out hymns one second, and then curse, lie, steal, and commit all types of unclean acts the next. This is as wrong as $2 + 2 = 7$; it just doesn't add up. Reciting scriptures eloquently, flawlessly performing religious rituals, and convincingly sounding saved will not cut it. Christianity is not about "performing" on Sunday or at special events; it is about ministering and living an upright life, regardless of the day of the week or who is looking.

Several years ago, I was at work, and my supervisor and I were talking about church folks acting this way one minute and that way the next. My supervisor was saying that it humors him to see people that profess to be saved putting on holy airs and testifying at church, yet acting and speaking completely different in the workplace or in social settings. This constitutes being fake and is very unsafe! During our conversation, it was pointed out that we are the only Bible some people will ever read. As a result, we have to beware of our presentation of Christianity. As children of God, our representation of Him must be genuine or we will deter others from ever getting to know Him.

Not only does acting fake prevent us from sincerely working for God, but also fake behavior, actions, or items are just not the same as the "real" thing. Take synthetic hair- sure, it may enhance a person's appearance, but it just does not feel or look the same as human hair. Contact lenses surely enhance poor vision, but wearing them is not the same as having 20/20 eye sight. Purchasing dentures will assist an individual with chewing food or even enhance an unattractive smile, but from what I have been told, they do not feel as comfortable as the real teeth that grow in one's mouth. Face it-there is nothing like the "real thing!" This holds true in our attitudes, worship, and praise toward God.

Another thing I have learned about being and acting fake is that it leads to defeat. How, you may ask? Ponder this: two actors are auditioning for the same role. The first actor takes the script and immediately jumps into character, transmitting the lines; however, he does not arouse any emotions within the director and does not seem believable. The second actor takes the script, skims the lines briefly, and then assumes the identity of the character.

Actor two begins communicating the lines in a most believable way. The director becomes stirred up and overwhelmed with contentment because of the dramatic expression. Needless to say, actor one, because his performance felt phony, was not chosen for the production. If we act fake in our mannerisms, words, and actions, at some point, we will suffer defeat. Romantic ties are severed due to someone acting fake. Friendships have been destroyed due to someone being insincere. Because of the shams and "shows" that go on in some of our churches today, potential converts have been lost. I don't know about you, but just these examples alone are enough to make me work harder at being genuine in all things.

Finally, being fake is like being in bondage. One is limited, restricted, and cannot experience all that God has for him or her. John 8:32 states, "Then you will know the truth and the truth will make you free" (NIV). In truth, there is freedom; however, if one doesn't deal in the truth, there is no way he or she will experience its freedom. Therefore, if this is an area you need to work on, do so; God will be with you and guide you through. While you are working on improving in this area, bear in mind John 8:36, which proclaims, "So if the Son sets you free, you will be free indeed" (NIV). This scripture is assurance of the type of liberation God can bring about through His son, Jesus.

8 ONE-NIGHT STAND

While at work one day, I received one of my usual daily inspirational emails; this one discussed our relationships with people and things. Basically, the email stated that many times in our lives we find ourselves in admiration of things, people, and places. We act like we cannot live without these people, places, and objects. The writer goes on to say that, regarding our marriages and other relationships, there is an abundance of love and trust. In these relationships, it seems as though the more we are with our special someone, be it a spouse, significant other, child, or sibling, the harder it is for us to leave his or her presence. This email further discusses our admiration for our cars, homes, and jobs; according to the author, whatever the object of admiration may be, we find ourselves engulfed in it and always thinking about it. There are times when we daydream about it and cannot imagine life without it.

I must agree that this email was dead on. Take my sister and me: my younger sister and I are best friends and I love and trust her. We are buddies for real, and I can honestly say that I would have a hard time imagining my life without her in it. We talk every day, sometimes, all throughout the day. We may chat via text messages, phone conversations, or email but, one way or another, we communicate on a daily basis. Why? It is because this is important to us; we have a strong relationship, a tight bond. Likewise, I can say the same thing about my relationship with my spouse and my parents. My parents and I do not miss a day talking to each other, even if we have already seen each other that day. My spouse and I see each other day after day and still communicate on the phone daily. Why? It is because I love my family members and want to spend time with them. This is precisely how our relationship with God should be. We profess to be in His family; we claim to love Him. Why then is not our relationship with Him even remotely close to the tight-knit relationships we have with our loved ones and friends?

Time and time again people say, "Relationships take work." In order to build a strong relationship with anyone, it takes time, effort, and willingness. You must be willing to do the work, take time to do the work, and be compassionate and energetic about doing the work. If not, the relationship will not be strong, durable, and firm. There will not be a high level of trust, loyalty, or commitment. This holds true of our relationship with God. Can you confidently say your association with God is durable? Do you communicate with Him daily? Is your relationship with Him extremely important to you? If the answer to any of the above questions is, "No," then your bond with God should be re-evaluated. It must be treasured and honored, and should definitely not be treated like a one-night stand.

One-night stands, in my opinion, can best be summed up as embarrassing and awkward. I am sure you have seen television shows that depict humiliated characters that have participated in a one-night stand. Usually the characters feel cheap and used afterwards. Many times, one individual says of the other one, "He/She didn't even call me the next day!" How terrible is that? You gave of yourself to this person, and he or she doesn't even have the decency to call you the following day or any other day after that? Well, imagine how God must feel when countless numbers of us do the same? We use His goodness, partake of His blessings, breathe His air, and so on, but we cannot even thank Him, pray to Him, or spend time with Him? It seems like we are using Him, doesn't it?

Among church folks, it appears that "love" for God is not actually real love. Sometimes our love for Him does not look like the love that a child feels for a parent, or even how one friend feels about another friend. Our clouded concept of love for God seems more closely linked to infatuation, puppy love, or even a one-night stand. I say this because many of us know *of* God, but we don't really *know* Him. We have experienced Him from time to time, but this is due to *His* graciousness. We have felt His gentle hand on us occasionally, but this is due to *His* loving way. We have even talked to Him a time or two; most of the time this is attributed to us getting into trouble or feeling lonely.

Gospel artist, Brent Jones, and his group, T.P. Mobb, released a convicting song that causes one to really evaluate his or her relationship with God. Just in case you haven't figured it out yet, I love music! Anyway, in the song, the listener is basically warned not to wait until midnight to communicate with God. The song suggests that we routinely steal away from everything, including our Blackberry phones or iPhones, reality television shows, sports games, or whatever else takes up our time, and seek God. The song goes on to say that some of us are strangers to God until things start going wrong in our lives, and then we come running. We know that calling on anyone, especially God, only when it is beneficial to us, is not right.

This type of communication does not establish a proper relationship; it illustrates a broken, disjointed, and weak one. It is a one-sided relationship that cannot possibly be based on love.

A true Christian knows that, in order to establish a solid relationship and resilient bond with God, real time must be put in. It is not enough for us to vocally proclaim love for him, but spiritually and emotionally have no attachment to Him. Lip service is one thing, but action is another, and we all know that "love" is an action word. Love is an intangible concept, but is delivered through concrete actions. One can see, feel, and is aware of where and when true love abides.

The basis for Christianity is love; God is love and Jesus lived, preached, and taught love. Christianity is a way of life; it is not simply a set of beliefs to be confined within the walls of a church building. This is a lifestyle, not just a temporary task that is to be carried out only on Sunday mornings. This lifestyle is to be genuine and should be taken seriously; it is a way of life that should not be played with. Christianity is not to be attended to when one gets in the mood to "act saved" or when time permits. It should definitely not be the "thing to do" because someone else is doing it or because it looks right. It is ongoing and Christians should continuously grow and mature spiritually. The way to fully start embracing this lifestyle is to spend time reading, meditating, and getting to know God. You will surely fall in love with Him or else fall even more in love with Him!

Church folks tend to pick God up when it is convenient for them and drop Him the minute He is no longer needed. The problem is that He is always needed; we can't do anything without God! Furthermore, why would we want to? People affiliated with the church of God should always want to know and feel the love of God, the hand of God, and the presence of God. God is necessary! In the Bible, many of the psalms exhibit this truth. An awesome example can be found in the forty-second psalm. In the first and second verse it is stated, "As the deer pants for streams of water, so my soul pants for you, O God. My soul thirsts for God, for the living God" (NIV). Within this same text, the writer goes on to ask, "Where can I go and meet with God?" This individual is seeking God; He wants to be wherever God is. He even shares that his tears have been his food day and night while men constantly ask of him, "Where is your God?" This is similar to how a love sick individual feels when he or she has not talked to or seen his or her love interest for an extended amount of time.

A second instance can be found in the eighty-ninth psalm. Ethan, the Ezrahite wrote, "I will sing of the Lord's great love forever; with my mouth I will make your faithfulness known through all generations" (NIV). This verse alone should make you love God! As we already know, forever means just that; it is infinite and has no end. This is how the Lord's love is for us. It continues and continues and continues. No matter how we stray away, His love continues. Regardless of how many commandments we break, His love continues. Despite the fact that we are sinful, His love continues. Not only that, it is revealed that the Lord is faithful. Faithfulness is defined as exactness or consistent loyalty. Who does not want to be a part of this kind of relationship?

A third example can be found in the eighty-eighth psalm. The first verse states, "Lord, you are the God who saves me; day and night I cry out to you" (NIV). This is deep; day and night indicates continual crying out to God. If this writer cries out before God for hours on top of hours, or day and night, then God is obviously on his mind. To do anything day and night takes up all of one's time; obviously, this author does not mind putting in the time. I wonder why it is so hard for us to simply focus on God and give Him a couple of hours of our time just on Sunday alone? It is because we tend to treat this relationship like a one-night stand and not like the loving, faithful relationship it is intended to be.

An excellent depiction of a loving, devoted relationship with God is evident through David and God's interaction. David and God constantly communicated with each other because this was important to David and pleasing to God. Psalm 61:2 relays, "From the ends of the earth I call to you, I call as my heart grows faint" (NIV). He goes on to say, "I long to dwell in your tent forever and take refuge in the shelter of your wings" (NIV). David seemed to always want to draw near to God and he yearned for God to draw near to Him. This nearness was mandatory, necessary, and fulfilling to him. For David, spending time with God was a daily pleasure; sharing intimate, quality time with God was at the top of his list. Can we even say spending time with God is on our list at all?

There are so many scriptures that validate the

relationship between God and David. Psalm 17:8 reads, "Keep me as the apple of your eye; hide me in the shadow of your wings" (NIV). To be the apple of someone's eye is a privilege; it is flattering. Apparently, David was well aware of this because it was his prayer to remain the apple of God's eye. Also, David proclaimed his love for God aloud; he wasn't ashamed of his feelings for God. Psalm 18:1-2 relays, "I will love thee, Oh Lord, my strength" (KJV). David further reveals, "The Lord is my rock, and my fortress, and my deliverer; my God, my strength, in whom I will trust" (KJV). These scriptures are beautiful depictions of an authentic, loving union.

David knew that he had a good thing going with God and didn't want to do anything to mess up the relationship they built. Can we say the same thing of our relationship with God? Do we even have a meaningful relationship with Him? What I have found to be true is that we wait until we go through our "valley experiences" or when "midnight" sneaks up on us to begin talking to our Father. This is baffling to me because we always talk to and spend time with those we love; every day we communicate with our loved ones in some kind of way. It should be no different when it comes to God. If we truly love Him, then why are our relationships with Him so rocky?

The concept of reciprocity is one main reason the relationship between the Lord and David was so strong. This was not a one-sided relationship because both parties gave and took. David gave by praising God constantly and always attempting to do what was commanded of him. It is a known fact that he messed up and faltered at times, but, even in these cases, he fasted, prayed, and repented in order to maintain what was built between him and the Lord. In turn, God granted David the blessings, love, and safety he requested. Psalm 61:7-8 states, "May he (the King) be enthroned in God's presence forever…then will I ever sing praise to your name and fulfill my vows day after day" (NIV). This is part of our problem: we want what we want and we take and take, but have no intention of giving back in return. This is surely not real love.

I will conclude this chapter with some of the lyrics from Mary J. Blige's song, "Real Love." In this song, Blige sings, "Real love, I'm searching for a real love, someone to set my heart free." In one of her verses, she says, "I've been searching for someone to satisfy my every need; won't you be my inspiration, be the real love that I need?"

This was one of the most popular songs of the nineties, and rightfully so. Who wouldn't want a love like this? Well, I have great news for you: God has and is that real love! He has set us free, is our inspiration, and is as real as it gets. If you are like me and are steadily growing in the realization of God's love, it is not too late to fully start embracing it as well as reciprocating it. You can start by devoting more time to Him and getting more engrossed in His word. This way you will get to know Him better, experience Him more, and love Him greatly because to *know* Him *is* to *love* Him.

9 WHAT'S IN YOU?

While watching television, at some point throughout the day, the credit card company, Capital One, will air its commercial. In this commercial, you are asked, "What's in your wallet?" This is a very catchy slogan that grabs your attention. This question may invoke a little thought or make you snicker like it does to me; often times, I jokingly answer the question with, "Not much." Well, in this chapter I hope to raise some thought on what is really inside of *you*. This may not be fun, but, as stated in the second chapter, we are instructed to examine ourselves. Only then will we be able to identify the ungodly characteristics and unattractive attributes that thwart us from resembling Christ.

You have probably heard the statement, "What is in you will come out of you." This is a realistic declaration. A pastor that I know once said, "If someone steps on your toe and it hurts badly enough, what you really feel will come out of your mouth." He is so right; what you think and what is really stored up inside of you will spill out. Sometimes, this is not a good thing. Romans 7:18 states, "For I know that in me (that is, in my flesh,) dwelleth no good thing: for to will is present with me; but *how* to perform that which is good I find not" (KJV). As I admitted earlier, there is no way we can be good; our nature is sinful, but our God is able. Through the power of God, our sinful natures can be conquered. For we know, according to Ephesians 3:20, that God "is able to do exceeding, abundantly above all that we ask or think, according to the power that worketh in us" (KJV).

In order to allow God to do any work in us, we must operate in a spiritual mindset. By doing so, we can fully recognize the awesome power of our Father. Renowned gospel music artist, Donald Lawrence, wrote a song entitled "Your Righteous Mind." A line of this awesome song says "Let go of your natural thinking and embrace your righteous mind." From what I gather, the basis for this song stems from one of my mother's favorite scriptures: Philippians 4:8. This scripture says, "Finally, brethren, whatsoever things are true, whatsoever things are honest, whatsoever things are just, whatsoever things are pure, whatsoever things are lovely, whatsoever things are of good report; if there be any virtue, and if there be any praise, think on these things" (KJV). In reading these words, a picture of splendor and beauty is painted in my mind. This scripture gives off a sense of peace and tranquility; we should feel a pleasant calm about us after reading this. Splendor, tranquility, and peace are characteristics that can be attached to the person of Jesus Christ. In order to achieve this calmness, experience this beauty, and enjoy this peace, we have to meditate daily on the right things so that when the time comes, the right things will spill out of us.

A righteous mindset equals a spiritual mindset because, in the flesh, most of the time, we do not think righteously. Paul explains this best in the seventh chapter of Romans. He points out that he does not fully understand himself and his sinful way. Paul narrates to us his wishes to do good things and be good; however, this is impossible because his sinful nature causes him to be a slave to the law of sin. According to Romans 7:21, he admits, "So I find this law at work: although I want to do good, evil is right there with me" (NIV). You may find yourself agreeing with Paul; it seems like the desire to do right is there, yet we more easily give in to the evil that is always present. He does go on to state, in the twenty-second verse, "For in my inner being I delight in God's law" (NIV). This statement elucidates the importance of the inner self-mind, spirit, and soul. It is internally that

God looks and spiritually that we should operate. Paul concludes this chapter by celebrating God and then announcing in the twenty-fifth verse, "So then, I myself, in my mind, am a slave to God's law" (NIV).

Now, you may be asking yourself how to avoid becoming or continuing on as a slave to the law of sin. You may even be saying to yourself, "I read devotionals and a couple of chapters of the Bible each night; I read and hear the right things so some good should automatically flow out of me." This is not quite the case! We have got to do much more in order to be fully suited up to overcome each test and obstacle that will be thrown our way. We have to truly meditate on scriptures, follow the instructions that scriptures provide, and apply each principle to our everyday lives. We seem to forget that others, particularly the unsaved, are reading us like a book; be mindful that we may be the closest Bible some individuals will ever come in contact with!

Please do not get me wrong, exchanging inspirational emails with others and reading daily is good; however, it is just not enough. To bring this point a little closer to home for you, I would like to share a true situation. I attempt to read at least two chapters of the

Bible nightly and send and receive devotional messages several times a day; I thought I was doing pretty well consuming good, just, lovely, and pure things- until one particular Friday. I received a letter in the mail informing me that I was not selected for a position that I was so confident that I would get. What was inside of me then came rushing out!

Immediately after receiving the letter, my whole demeanor changed, and my attitude became less than pleasing. I began complaining about how unfair this was and how I did not appreciate the interview committee wasting my time and gas if they were not going to select me. I whimpered about how I met all of the qualifications and fussed about how people land jobs based on who they know instead of what they know; I was HOT! My ranting and raving led me into an ungrateful mode of thinking; in my mind, I started going over what I did not have in comparison to what others did have, how my career sucks in comparison to other people's, and so forth. This behavior was not an accurate representation of a true Christian; I say this because complaining, whining, and ungratefulness are attributes Jesus cannot take credit for possessing.

There are great instances recorded in the Bible that illustrate this point. In the sixth chapter of Mark, Jesus, along with His disciples, was tired and hungry as a result of teaching and healing multitudes of people. As they were trying to steal away to a quiet place to rest, a new multitude of people saw Jesus and his men leaving; they ran to catch up with them. Instead of huffing and puffing in annoyance, the thirty-fourth verse indicates that Jesus "had compassion on them," whereas he could have whined about how exhausted and famished He was (NIV).

Another instance, found in the seventeenth chapter of Luke, describes the parable of the ten lepers. You know the story: ten lepers met Jesus as He was going into a village. From a distance, they called out, "Jesus, Master, have pity on us!" (Luke 17:11, NIV). He did. After healing them, they went on their way, yet only one of the ten turned back to show his appreciation. Jesus asked, "Were not all ten cleansed? Where are the other nine? Has no one returned to give praise to God except this foreigner?" (Luke 17:17-18, NIV). Had He gotten an attitude with the lepers and complained about how ungrateful they were, this would have been understandable, don't you think? However, He let the situation rest and did not waste time complaining because it was what it was! Also, this just portrays the exemplary model we should follow.

One final example I would like to share is that of Jesus' sacrifice. When He sacrificed His life to atone for our sins, He could have whined, complained, and yelled. While on the cross, looking over the hostile crowd of the many familiar people He had ministered to, laid hands on, and cared so much for, he could have started murmuring about how ungrateful and undeserving we are. Of course, He did not mumble one word while hanging on the cross dying a selfless death for us.

At all times, the right things flowed from Jesus. Yes, I know-we are not perfect like Him. Again, I repeat, we must try as hard as possible to mirror His image. So, how do we ensure that the right things come out of us as much as possible? We get into the right mindset, encircle ourselves with the right people, and surround ourselves with the right things. In order to get into the right mindset, we must be willing to de-clutter our minds of mess, drama, and free ourselves of the litter we carry around. Also, it is so necessary for us to continuously fill ourselves up with the goodness of God through music, scriptures, sermons, and the company of other Christians. We should want to ensure that we model the godliest lifestyle humanly possible.

Another way to ensure that righteousness spills out of us is to continuously speak correctly and repeatedly do good things. Let us take a glimpse at the words written in Matthew 12: 34-35. Here we find that Jesus asks, "You brood of vipers, how can you who are evil say anything good? He goes on to say, "For the mouth speaks what the heart is full of" (NIV). If you really look at this scripture, you will find that it is pretty cut and dry. If you do not practice doing good things and seek after goodness, you cannot possible speak anything good. It is reiterated here that whatever is flowing in your heart will flow right out of your mouth. According to Jesus, the good man brings good things out of the good stored up in him, and the evil man brings evil things out of the evil stored up in him.

Additionally, to ensure we do not eject the wrong ideas, motives, words, and deeds, we must bear in mind the words "decent" and "holy." In 1 Corinthians 14:40, it is said, "Let all things be done decently and in order" (KJV). Things done decently and orderly are done right and appropriately. This is just how God operates and how He is.

The terms "decent" and "holy" are two important words that Moses shares with the Israelites, in somewhat of a "farewell address" to them. In Deuteronomy 23:14, the people of Israel are told, "For the Lord your God moves about in your camp to protect you and to deliver your enemies to you. Your camp must be holy, so that He will not see among you anything indecent and turn away from you" (NIV). It would be a disaster if God turns away from us due to indecency and an absence of holiness. We know it would be a disastrous situation, because there are several biblical accounts we can take note of. One account is the destruction of Sodom and Gomorrah. This place was extremely sinful, taking pleasure in arrogance, committing sexually indecent acts, and showing no regard for the law, to name a few sins. In Genesis 19:12, the angels of the Lord state, "The outcry to the Lord against its people is so great that he has sent us to destroy it" (NIV).

A second account can be found in the book of Jonah. According to Jonah 1:2, God instructs Jonah to "Arise, go to Nineveh, that great city, and cry against it; for their wickedness is come up before me" (KJV). You know the story: Jonah, after being disobedient, finally arrived in Nineveh and did as he was commanded. However, the people of the city heard what God was saying through the prophet; they believed, proclaimed a fast, and repented. As a result of their decent, orderly repentance, God's anger subsided. This biblical account illustrates the fact that the right things do not always come out of us; however, if we possess compassionate hearts, speak kind words, perform unselfish deeds, repent when we sin, and try our best to live holy and decent lives, we can be sure that we will not see one day of destruction.

10 THE WINNING SIDE

Around 2012, I had to start talking to my oldest daughter about getting so discouraged and upset when she does not win something. She is very competitive when it comes to playing board and electronic games; when she does not win, her whole demeanor changes. After she loses a game, she, all of a sudden, doesn't want to play anymore. She whimpers, whines, and pouts; sometimes, she goes into her room and sits in silence for a little while. Of course, part of this immature behavior is due to her young age; however, regardless of age, we all want to win!

Every day we hear different tales of individuals who want to win. Some people buy tickets in hopes of winning a lottery. Some people go to casinos in hopes of winning at table games or on slot machines. Some companies advertise services and products with hopes of winning over customers. Some young ladies enter beauty pageants in hopes of winning a title. Politicians broadcast their campaign commercials and slogans in hopes of winning an elected position. Students conduct school campaigns to receive votes from their peers in areas of student government or races for the titles of "Best Dressed," "Most Beautiful," and "Most Likely to Succeed." Sports and athletics teams play hard all season in hopes of winning a championship and/or title. I mean, who does not like to win?

It should go without saying that, in order to win, there must be preparation. Countless hours must be spent honing our crafts, refining our talents, strengthening our muscles, developing our skills, and building up our stamina. We have to be strategic and methodical, crafty and creative, and motivated and driven to achieve victory. In doing so, success will surely be within our grasps. On the flip side, being ill-prepared, incompetent, or weak in spirit, mind, or heart will, without question, lead to defeat. A true victor is not faint at heart, physically weak, or mentally incompetent. He or she is always up for the challenge and hungry for victory.

The concept of winning is viewed differently by each individual. To each of us, winning may mean something different; however, we each love the feeling of basking in victory! To an educator, winning may mean that all students pass to the next grade at the end of the school year. To a politician, winning may mean securing an elected position in government. To a child, winning may mean getting a parent to buy a toy. To a single woman, winning may mean getting married. To a childless man, winning may mean fathering a son. To a musician, winning may be the release of a project to the public. To an artist, winning may be having artwork displayed in a distinguished art gallery. To a chef, winning may mean landing a cooking television show. To a recent law school graduate, winning may mean securing a position at a prestigious firm. To a pastor, winning may mean a huge boost in attendance on Sunday. Regardless of profession, gender, or age, we all prefer winning over losing.

As a Christian, winning should be important. There is definitely nothing wrong with wanting to win. The question is what does winning really mean and how important is it to God? We should consider how God looks at achievement and then determine if we measure victory in the same way. Some individuals measure success by how many church programs they have chaired. Others measure success by how many members of the congregation know their names. Do you measure victory by how often your name gets called aloud? Just what constitutes winning in your eyes? I do believe our successes must be measurable by God's standards.

God's standards do not include anything worldly.

As aforementioned, God looks at our hearts and deeds. He is not impressed by how many program bulletins our names are printed in or how many solos we lead. He is unconcerned about how long we pray or how much money we give (except our ten percent and cheerful offerings, of course). He is not moved by how loud we shout or how hard we dance. He is not mesmerized by how many people say, "Amen" when we preach or speak. He cares about how many souls we try to help, how we treat each other, and how much we love Him. Ultimately, He is concerned with whose side of this spiritual war you are on.

The way church folks are acting these days it is hard to tell who is on God's side and who is not. Too many of us are displaying those ungodly traits mentioned in chapter three. We cause chaos in the church instead of encouraging harmony. We get more excited by the choir "performing" than the sinner who accepts Christ when the doors of the church are opened. We criticize more than we motivate. We tend to point out the wrong in everybody, yet forget that we are full of wrong also. We continuously make excuses instead of improvements. These things have got to be corrected or else the church will continue lacking in its zeal, and its light will keep dwindling. We have got to get serious about doing better and we have got to be excited about it!

Imagine that you are at a football game; you are pumped and ready for a thrilling next couple of hours. You are dressed in your paraphernalia with your pom-pom in hand. When you take your place in the stands, whether sitting or standing, most likely you are going to sit on the side of the team you are there to support. In your eyes, this is the winning team, right? If you are a home-body, you may choose to stay home and watch the game from the privacy of your own home. You cheer, jump, yell, root, clap, or even dance for your favorite team. Why do you do all of this? It is because you have invested in this team, be it time, money, energy, or emotion. You want this team to win.

As a Christian, this is exactly how we should feel about our team. We are a team of believers, encouragers, motivators, peacemakers, and servants. Just as a professional football team works hard all season to get to the Super Bowl, we are to work our entire lives to get to heaven. Just as a high school cheerleading squad practices after school during the week, we are to practice living justly and righteously every day. In the same manner that a serious athlete eats right and exercises daily, we are to partake of spiritual food and exercise godliness. Just as teams suit up in their game attire to come out and play a game, we are to put on the whole armor of God in order to withstand the evil plots of the enemy. We are to devote time, energy, resources, and whatever is necessary, to ensure our team is successful. If we work together, just as any other team, we can accomplish much and become champions.

We already have the victory through Christ Jesus; we cannot lose! We do not have to fear defeat or worry about being overthrown. We do not have to be afraid of anyone or anything; we are victorious! Roman 8:37 reminds us that, "Nay, in all these things, we are more than conquerors through Him that loved us" (KJV). This alone should be enough to motivate, energize, and inspire you to righteously, powerfully fight the good fight. If this is not enough motivation to stir you up, 1 Corinthians 15:57 says, "But thanks be to God; He gives us the victory through our Lord Jesus Christ" (NIV).

Now that we have reached the end of this journey, can you honestly admit that you see some things differently? Have you taken a nice, long look at yourself?

Are there any areas of your Christian walk you now plan to improve? As stated in the opening chapter, I do not profess to know it all and I definitely did not try to come across as a "holy roller." I feel a lot like Paul when he stated in Philippians 3:12, "Not that I have already obtained all this, or have already been made perfect, but I press on to take hold of that which Christ Jesus took hold of me" (KJV). I am nowhere close to perfect and there is still much I do not know or understand about Christianity, but, what I have gained an understanding of throughout the course of my life, I have tried to share with you here.

As we go forward, moving from *doing* church to *living* as Christ, let us do as Paul instructs and, "forgetting those things which are behind, and reaching forth unto those things which are before, let us press toward the mark for the prize of the high calling of God in Christ Jesus" (Philippians 3:13-14, KJV). Remember, in the end, only one side is going to win. In order to be victorious, we must be real. Also, it is imperative that we invest our time and energy into what actually matters-faithfully, truthfully, and wholeheartedly serving God. We should elect to not continue half-worshipping, half-loving, half-serving, or half-doing *anything*. We should vow to be better, live, love, and serve better, and not give in to the attitudes and negativity of our flesh. If you really aspire to improve in any way, as you close this book, think on the following words from Dr. Krejcir:

> Remember, churches fail because we place our needs and desires over the Lord's. It is His Church and we are His people. Let our focus be on the right target—that is, His and not ours! We are called to a higher purpose. We are not called to ourselves. Ministry is a dangerous thing because we are before a Holy God. Yes, we have grace, but we have responsibility too (2007).

We, authentic Christians, have a responsibility to represent Christ. We should no longer be complacent behaving immaturely, thinking selfishly, or acting indecently. We are in it to win it! We are to win souls for Christ, and we can do it. I can confidently declare this because we are members of God's royal family and true ambassadors for Christ. If you really believe this, there is nothing left to do except exhibit this. Now is a great time to decide who you would rather resemble: one of those church folks or a genuine Christian.

WORKS CITED

"Census Bureau Homepage." *Census Bureau Homepage.* N.p., n.d. Web. 6 July 2012.

"Global Christianity - A Report on the Size and Distribution of the World's Christian Population - Pew Forum on Religion & Public Life." *Pew Research Center*, 19 Dec. 2011. Web. 4 Sept. 2012.

Hill, Dale. "B.U.S.Y." *Practical Bible Teaching.* N.p., n.d. Web. 20 Jan. 2012.

Krejcir, Richard, Ph. D. "Statistics and Reasons for Church Decline." *Into Thy Word Ministries.* The Francis A. Schaeffer Institute, 2007. Web. 5 July 2012.

ABOUT THE AUTHOR

Michelle Coleman Anderson is a native of Jackson, Mississippi. She is the happy wife of Gussie Anderson, and together they have four unique and hilarious children. She is a proud member of St. Luther Missionary Baptist Church, under the former leadership of Rev. Dr. Charles E. Polk, Sr., and the current leadership of Rev. Charles E. Polk, Jr. She formerly served as Minister of Music/Pianist at several local churches in the Jackson Metropolitan area. Currently, she serves in music ministry at New Era M.B. Church. Regarding education, Michelle holds an undergraduate and graduate degree from Hinds Community College and Troy University, and an undergraduate and graduate degree in English from Jackson State University. She is currently pursuing a doctoral degree in Leadership from the University of the Cumberlands. Professionally, she currently leads a nonprofit organization in Hancock County, Mississippi, and serves as an adjunct instructor of English at Colorado Christian University. She enjoys writing, reading, playing the piano, watching tennis matches, and, most of all, spending quality time with her amazing family.

Made in the USA
Coppell, TX
13 February 2026

72038039R00066